# SET GOALS
# PLAN FOOD
# GET SLEEP
# DRINK WATER
# EXERCISE
# REPEAT

## CONTACT US

We'd love to hear from you!
Send us your questions, feedback and requests for
new journal designs and layouts.

Email: SunshinePressPub@gmail.com

**Three months from now, you will thank yourself.**

# weight tracker

| DATE | WEIGHT | DATE | WEIGHT |
| --- | --- | --- | --- |
| | | | |
| | | | |
| | | | |
| | | | |
| | | | |
| | | | |
| | | | |
| | | | |
| | | | |
| | | | |
| | | | |
| | | | |
| | | | |
| | | | |
| | | | |
| | | | |
| | | | |
| | | | |
| | | | |
| | | | |
| | | | |
| | | | |
| | | | |
| | | | |
| | | | |
| | | | |
| | | | |

# goals

ONE YEAR GOAL

## MONTH ONE

WEEKLY:

## MONTH TWO

WEEKLY:

## MONTH THREE

WEEKLY:

# daily journal *sample*

## WHAT WENT WELL YESTERDAY?

-Went out for a walk even though it was rainy.
-Skipped morning snack because I wasn't actually hungry.
-Ordered planned nonfat latte instead of mocha that sounded good.

## WHAT WENT POORLY YESTERDAY?

Wasn't really hungry all day, then was STARVING while cooking dinner. Had several bites of kids' food + pieces cheese out of the fridge.

## WHAT CAN I IMPROVE?

Plan some no/low calories snacks to have late afternoon/while cooking dinner. Celery/Cucumber/tomato w/ salt and pepper?

## ON MY MIND TODAY...

Feeling stressed about going to husband's work party next week. I wish I started losing weight earlier, but there's nothing I can do to change that now. I'm happy I've lost 10 pounds so far, but sometimes my goal weight feels so far away. I wish I could meet his coworkers when I'm at my best. I just don't want to wonder if he's embarrassed about how I look. Normally I'd just eat whatever to "make myself feel better," but I am learning that food doesn't solve any problems... especially when it only makes my goal farther away! I bet if I go shopping for a new dress that flatters my size NOW, I'll feel better about going. Maybe I'll get my hair colored, too. I just want to feel CONFIDENT, and I hate that I let food get in the way of that. I want to keep planning my food and exercising so that I don't carry stress like this anymore.

# daily plan *sample*

## AFFIRMATION

Stop letting food be the boss of you!

## SLEEP    7 hours

## WATER

X X X X X̄ X X 8 9 10

## GOALS

-drink all my water!
-leave 2+ bites at lunch
-no bites of kids' snacks

## EXERCISE

30 min trail walk +
15min pilates video

| 24 HOUR PLAN | | ACTUAL |
|---|---|---|
| **B** coffee with cream, clio bar, oatmeal w/ raspberries | ✓ | |
| **L** grilled chicken sandwich + side salad (dining out) | ☐ | 1/2 cheeseburger, side salad + a few french fries |
| **D** 4oz pork tenderloin, cauliflower mash, green beans | ✓ | |
| **S** AM - apple w/ PB2  PM- 2 sugar free popsicles | ✓ | |

## NOTES

Lunch w/ Whitney. Planned eating chicken sandwich on my own, but she wanted to split a burger. Seemed like a good compromise, and I still ate a side salad!

# daily journal

WHAT WENT WELL YESTERDAY?

WHAT WENT POORLY YESTERDAY?

WHAT CAN I IMPROVE?

## ON MY MIND TODAY...

_____
_____
_____
_____
_____
_____
_____
_____
_____
_____
_____
_____

# daily plan

DATE

| AFFIRMATION | SLEEP |
| | |
| | WATER |
| | 1 2 3 4 5 6 7 8 9 10 |
| GOALS | EXERCISE |
| | |

| 24 HOUR PLAN | ACTUAL |
| --- | --- |
| B | |
| L | |
| D | |
| S | |

NOTES

# daily journal

**WHAT WENT WELL YESTERDAY?**

**WHAT WENT POORLY YESTERDAY?**

**WHAT CAN I IMPROVE?**

## ON MY MIND TODAY...

_____
_____
_____
_____
_____
_____
_____
_____
_____
_____
_____
_____
_____
_____

# daily plan

DATE

| AFFIRMATION | SLEEP |
| | WATER |
| | 1 2 3 4 5 6 7 8 9 10 |
| GOALS | EXERCISE |

| 24 HOUR PLAN | ACTUAL |
|---|---|
| B | ☐ |
| L | ☐ |
| D | ☐ |
| S | ☐ |

NOTES

# daily journal

**WHAT WENT WELL YESTERDAY?**


**WHAT WENT POORLY YESTERDAY?**


**WHAT CAN I IMPROVE?**


**ON MY MIND TODAY...**

_____
_____
_____
_____
_____
_____
_____
_____
_____
_____
_____
_____

# daily plan

**AFFIRMATION**

**SLEEP**

**WATER**

1　2　3　4　5　6　7　8　9　10

**GOALS**

**EXERCISE**

| 24 HOUR PLAN | ACTUAL |
|:---:|:---:|
| **B** ☐ | |
| **L** ☐ | |
| **D** ☐ | |
| **S** ☐ | |

**NOTES**

# daily journal

**WHAT WENT WELL YESTERDAY?**




**WHAT WENT POORLY YESTERDAY?**




**WHAT CAN I IMPROVE?**




**ON MY MIND TODAY...**

_____
_____
_____
_____
_____
_____
_____
_____
_____
_____
_____
_____
_____

# daily plan

DATE

| AFFIRMATION | SLEEP |
| | WATER |
| | 1 2 3 4 5 6 7 8 9 10 |
| GOALS | EXERCISE |

| 24 HOUR PLAN | ACTUAL |
|---|---|
| B | |
| L | |
| D | |
| S | |

NOTES

# daily journal

**WHAT WENT WELL YESTERDAY?**

**WHAT WENT POORLY YESTERDAY?**

**WHAT CAN I IMPROVE?**

**ON MY MIND TODAY...**

_____
_____
_____
_____
_____
_____
_____
_____
_____
_____
_____
_____

# daily plan

DATE

AFFIRMATION

SLEEP

WATER

1 2 3 4 5 6 7 8 9 10

GOALS

EXERCISE

| 24 HOUR PLAN | ACTUAL |
|---|---|
| B | |
| L | |
| D | |
| S | |

NOTES

# daily journal

**WHAT WENT WELL YESTERDAY?**

**WHAT WENT POORLY YESTERDAY?**

**WHAT CAN I IMPROVE?**

**ON MY MIND TODAY...**

_____

_____

_____

_____

_____

_____

_____

_____

_____

_____

_____

_____

_____

# daily plan

**AFFIRMATION**

**SLEEP**

**WATER**

1 2 3 4 5 6 7 8 9 10

**GOALS**

**EXERCISE**

| 24 HOUR PLAN | ACTUAL |
|---|---|
| B | |
| L | |
| D | |
| S | |

**NOTES**

# daily journal

**WHAT WENT WELL YESTERDAY?**


**WHAT WENT POORLY YESTERDAY?**


**WHAT CAN I IMPROVE?**


**ON MY MIND TODAY...**

_____
_____
_____
_____
_____
_____
_____
_____
_____
_____
_____
_____
_____

# daily plan

DATE

| AFFIRMATION | SLEEP |
| | WATER |
| | 1 2 3 4 5 6 7 8 9 10 |
| GOALS | EXERCISE |

| 24 HOUR PLAN | ACTUAL |
|---|---|
| B | |
| L | |
| D | |
| S | |

NOTES

# daily journal

**WHAT WENT WELL YESTERDAY?**

**WHAT WENT POORLY YESTERDAY?**

**WHAT CAN I IMPROVE?**

**ON MY MIND TODAY...**

_____
_____
_____
_____
_____
_____
_____
_____
_____
_____
_____
_____
_____
_____

# daily plan

| AFFIRMATION | SLEEP |
| --- | --- |
| | WATER |
| | 1 2 3 4 5 6 7 8 9 10 |
| GOALS | EXERCISE |

| 24 HOUR PLAN | ACTUAL |
| --- | --- |
| B | □ |
| L | □ |
| D | □ |
| S | □ |

NOTES

# daily journal

**WHAT WENT WELL YESTERDAY?**

**WHAT WENT POORLY YESTERDAY?**

**WHAT CAN I IMPROVE?**

**ON MY MIND TODAY...**

_____

_____

_____

_____

_____

_____

_____

_____

_____

_____

_____

_____

# daily plan

**DATE**

**AFFIRMATION**

**SLEEP**

**WATER**

1 2 3 4 5 6 7 8 9 10

**GOALS**

**EXERCISE**

| 24 HOUR PLAN | ACTUAL |
|---|---|
| B | |
| L | |
| D | |
| S | |

**NOTES**

# daily journal

**WHAT WENT WELL YESTERDAY?**

**WHAT WENT POORLY YESTERDAY?**

**WHAT CAN I IMPROVE?**

**ON MY MIND TODAY...**

_____
_____
_____
_____
_____
_____
_____
_____
_____
_____
_____
_____

# daily plan

DATE

**AFFIRMATION**

**SLEEP**

**WATER**

1 2 3 4 5 6 7 8 9 10

**GOALS**

**EXERCISE**

| 24 HOUR PLAN | ACTUAL |
|---|---|
| B | ☐ |
| L | ☐ |
| D | ☐ |
| S | ☐ |

**NOTES**

# daily journal

**WHAT WENT WELL YESTERDAY?**

**WHAT WENT POORLY YESTERDAY?**

**WHAT CAN I IMPROVE?**

**ON MY MIND TODAY...**

# daily plan

DATE

| AFFIRMATION | SLEEP |
| | WATER |
| | 1 2 3 4 5 6 7 8 9 10 |
| GOALS | EXERCISE |

| 24 HOUR PLAN | ACTUAL |
| --- | --- |
| B □ | |
| L □ | |
| D □ | |
| S □ | |

NOTES

# daily journal

**WHAT WENT WELL YESTERDAY?**

**WHAT WENT POORLY YESTERDAY?**

**WHAT CAN I IMPROVE?**

**ON MY MIND TODAY...**

# daily plan

**DATE**

| AFFIRMATION | SLEEP |
| | WATER |
| | 1 2 3 4 5 6 7 8 9 10 |
| GOALS | EXERCISE |

| 24 HOUR PLAN | ACTUAL |
| --- | --- |
| B | ☐ |
| L | ☐ |
| D | ☐ |
| S | ☐ |

**NOTES**

# daily journal

**WHAT WENT WELL YESTERDAY?**

**WHAT WENT POORLY YESTERDAY?**

**WHAT CAN I IMPROVE?**

**ON MY MIND TODAY...**

_____
_____
_____
_____
_____
_____
_____
_____
_____
_____
_____
_____
_____

# daily plan

DATE

| AFFIRMATION | SLEEP |
| --- | --- |
| | **WATER** |
| | 1 2 3 4 5 6 7 8 9 10 |
| **GOALS** | **EXERCISE** |

| 24 HOUR PLAN | ACTUAL |
| --- | --- |
| B | |
| L | |
| D | |
| S | |

NOTES

# daily journal

**WHAT WENT WELL YESTERDAY?**

**WHAT WENT POORLY YESTERDAY?**

**WHAT CAN I IMPROVE?**

### ON MY MIND TODAY...

_____

_____

_____

_____

_____

_____

_____

_____

_____

_____

_____

_____

_____

_____

# daily plan

DATE

| AFFIRMATION | SLEEP |
| | WATER |
| | 1 2 3 4 5 6 7 8 9 10 |
| GOALS | EXERCISE |

| 24 HOUR PLAN | ACTUAL |
| --- | --- |
| B ☐ | |
| L ☐ | |
| D ☐ | |
| S ☐ | |

NOTES

# daily journal

**WHAT WENT WELL YESTERDAY?**

**WHAT WENT POORLY YESTERDAY?**

**WHAT CAN I IMPROVE?**

**ON MY MIND TODAY...**

# daily plan

DATE

**AFFIRMATION**

**SLEEP**

**WATER**

1 2 3 4 5 6 7 8 9 10

**GOALS**

**EXERCISE**

| 24 HOUR PLAN | ACTUAL |
|---|---|
| **B** | |
| **L** | |
| **D** | |
| **S** | |

**NOTES**

# daily journal

**WHAT WENT WELL YESTERDAY?**

**WHAT WENT POORLY YESTERDAY?**

**WHAT CAN I IMPROVE?**

**ON MY MIND TODAY...**

# daily plan

DATE

**AFFIRMATION**

**SLEEP**

**WATER**

1 2 3 4 5 6 7 8 9 10

**GOALS**

**EXERCISE**

| 24 HOUR PLAN | ACTUAL |
|---|---|
| B | |
| L | |
| D | |
| S | |

**NOTES**

# daily journal

**WHAT WENT WELL YESTERDAY?**

**WHAT WENT POORLY YESTERDAY?**

**WHAT CAN I IMPROVE?**

**ON MY MIND TODAY...**

# daily plan

DATE

## AFFIRMATION

## SLEEP

## WATER

1 2 3 4 5 6 7 8 9 10

## GOALS

## EXERCISE

| 24 HOUR PLAN | ACTUAL |
|:---:|:---:|
| B ☐ | |
| L ☐ | |
| D ☐ | |
| S ☐ | |

## NOTES

# daily journal

**WHAT WENT WELL YESTERDAY?**

**WHAT WENT POORLY YESTERDAY?**

**WHAT CAN I IMPROVE?**

**ON MY MIND TODAY...**

# daily plan

DATE

**AFFIRMATION**

**SLEEP**

**WATER**

1 2 3 4 5 6 7 8 9 10

**GOALS**

**EXERCISE**

| 24 HOUR PLAN | ACTUAL |
|---|---|
| B | ☐ |
| L | ☐ |
| D | ☐ |
| S | ☐ |

**NOTES**

# daily journal

**WHAT WENT WELL YESTERDAY?**

**WHAT WENT POORLY YESTERDAY?**

**WHAT CAN I IMPROVE?**

**ON MY MIND TODAY...**

_____
_____
_____
_____
_____
_____
_____
_____
_____
_____
_____
_____
_____

# daily plan

DATE

AFFIRMATION

SLEEP

WATER

1 2 3 4 5 6 7 8 9 10

GOALS

EXERCISE

| 24 HOUR PLAN | ACTUAL |
|---|---|
| B | |
| L | |
| D | |
| S | |

NOTES

# daily journal

**WHAT WENT WELL YESTERDAY?**

**WHAT WENT POORLY YESTERDAY?**

**WHAT CAN I IMPROVE?**

**ON MY MIND TODAY...**

_____
_____
_____
_____
_____
_____
_____
_____
_____
_____
_____
_____
_____

# daily plan

DATE

**AFFIRMATION**

**SLEEP**

**WATER**

1 2 3 4 5 6 7 8 9 10

**GOALS**

**EXERCISE**

| 24 HOUR PLAN | ACTUAL |
|---|---|
| B | |
| L | |
| D | |
| S | |

**NOTES**

# daily journal

**WHAT WENT WELL YESTERDAY?**

**WHAT WENT POORLY YESTERDAY?**

**WHAT CAN I IMPROVE?**

**ON MY MIND TODAY...**

_____
_____
_____
_____
_____
_____
_____
_____
_____
_____
_____
_____
_____

# daily plan

| AFFIRMATION | SLEEP |
| --- | --- |
| | WATER |
| | 1 2 3 4 5 6 7 8 9 10 |
| GOALS | EXERCISE |

| 24 HOUR PLAN | ACTUAL |
| --- | --- |
| B | ☐ |
| L | ☐ |
| D | ☐ |
| S | ☐ |

**NOTES**

# daily journal

**WHAT WENT WELL YESTERDAY?**

**WHAT WENT POORLY YESTERDAY?**

**WHAT CAN I IMPROVE?**

**ON MY MIND TODAY...**

_____
_____
_____
_____
_____
_____
_____
_____
_____
_____
_____
_____
_____

# daily plan

| AFFIRMATION | SLEEP |
| --- | --- |
| | WATER |
| | 1 2 3 4 5 6 7 8 9 10 |
| GOALS | EXERCISE |

| 24 HOUR PLAN | ACTUAL |
| --- | --- |
| B | |
| L | |
| D | |
| S | |

NOTES

# daily journal

**WHAT WENT WELL YESTERDAY?**

**WHAT WENT POORLY YESTERDAY?**

**WHAT CAN I IMPROVE?**

**ON MY MIND TODAY...**

_____
_____
_____
_____
_____
_____
_____
_____
_____
_____
_____
_____
_____

# daily plan

DATE

**AFFIRMATION**

**SLEEP**

**WATER**

1 2 3 4 5 6 7 8 9 10

**GOALS**

**EXERCISE**

| 24 HOUR PLAN | ACTUAL |
|---|---|
| B | |
| L | |
| D | |
| S | |

**NOTES**

# daily journal

**WHAT WENT WELL YESTERDAY?**

**WHAT WENT POORLY YESTERDAY?**

**WHAT CAN I IMPROVE?**

**ON MY MIND TODAY...**

_____

_____

_____

_____

_____

_____

_____

_____

_____

_____

_____

_____

_____

_____

# daily plan

DATE

| AFFIRMATION | SLEEP |
|---|---|
| | WATER |
| | 1 2 3 4 5 6 7 8 9 10 |
| GOALS | EXERCISE |
| | |

| 24 HOUR PLAN | ACTUAL |
|---|---|
| B □ | |
| L □ | |
| D □ | |
| S □ | |

NOTES

# daily journal

**WHAT WENT WELL YESTERDAY?**

**WHAT WENT POORLY YESTERDAY?**

**WHAT CAN I IMPROVE?**

**ON MY MIND TODAY...**

# daily plan

| AFFIRMATION | SLEEP |
| | WATER |
| | 1 2 3 4 5 6 7 8 9 10 |
| GOALS | EXERCISE |

| 24 HOUR PLAN | ACTUAL |
| --- | --- |
| B | □ |
| L | □ |
| D | □ |
| S | □ |

NOTES

# daily journal

**WHAT WENT WELL YESTERDAY?**

**WHAT WENT POORLY YESTERDAY?**

**WHAT CAN I IMPROVE?**

**ON MY MIND TODAY...**

_____

_____

_____

_____

_____

_____

_____

_____

_____

_____

_____

_____

_____

# daily plan

**AFFIRMATION**

**SLEEP**

**WATER**

1 2 3 4 5 6 7 8 9 10

**GOALS**

**EXERCISE**

| 24 HOUR PLAN | ACTUAL |
|:---:|:---:|
| B | |
| L | |
| D | |
| S | |

**NOTES**

# daily journal

**WHAT WENT WELL YESTERDAY?**

**WHAT WENT POORLY YESTERDAY?**

**WHAT CAN I IMPROVE?**

**ON MY MIND TODAY...**

_____
_____
_____
_____
_____
_____
_____
_____
_____
_____
_____
_____

# daily plan

DATE

**AFFIRMATION**

**SLEEP**

**WATER**

1 2 3 4 5 6 7 8 9 10

**GOALS**

**EXERCISE**

| 24 HOUR PLAN | ACTUAL |
|:---:|:---:|
| **B** ☐ | |
| **L** ☐ | |
| **D** ☐ | |
| **S** ☐ | |

**NOTES**

# daily journal

**WHAT WENT WELL YESTERDAY?**

**WHAT WENT POORLY YESTERDAY?**

**WHAT CAN I IMPROVE?**

**ON MY MIND TODAY...**

_____
_____
_____
_____
_____
_____
_____
_____
_____
_____
_____
_____
_____
_____

# daily plan

DATE

AFFIRMATION

SLEEP

WATER

1 2 3 4 5 6 7 8 9 10

GOALS

EXERCISE

| 24 HOUR PLAN | ACTUAL |
|---|---|
| B | |
| L | |
| D | |
| S | |

NOTES

# daily journal

**WHAT WENT WELL YESTERDAY?**

**WHAT WENT POORLY YESTERDAY?**

**WHAT CAN I IMPROVE?**

## ON MY MIND TODAY...

_____
_____
_____
_____
_____
_____
_____
_____
_____
_____
_____
_____
_____
_____

# daily plan

**AFFIRMATION**

**SLEEP**

**WATER**

1 2 3 4 5 6 7 8 9 10

**GOALS**

**EXERCISE**

| 24 HOUR PLAN | ACTUAL |
|---|---|
| B | |
| L | |
| D | |
| S | |

**NOTES**

# daily journal

**WHAT WENT WELL YESTERDAY?**

**WHAT WENT POORLY YESTERDAY?**

**WHAT CAN I IMPROVE?**

### ON MY MIND TODAY...

_____

_____

_____

_____

_____

_____

_____

_____

_____

_____

_____

_____

_____

_____

_____

# daily plan

DATE

**AFFIRMATION**

**SLEEP**

**WATER**

1 2 3 4 5 6 7 8 9 10

**GOALS**

**EXERCISE**

| 24 HOUR PLAN | ACTUAL |
|---|---|
| B ☐ | |
| L ☐ | |
| D ☐ | |
| S ☐ | |

**NOTES**

# daily journal

**WHAT WENT WELL YESTERDAY?**

**WHAT WENT POORLY YESTERDAY?**

**WHAT CAN I IMPROVE?**

**ON MY MIND TODAY...**

_____
_____
_____
_____
_____
_____
_____
_____
_____
_____
_____
_____

# daily plan

**DATE**

| AFFIRMATION | SLEEP |
| --- | --- |
| | **WATER** |
| | 1 2 3 4 5 6 7 8 9 10 |

| GOALS | EXERCISE |
| --- | --- |

| 24 HOUR PLAN | ACTUAL |
| --- | --- |
| B □ | |
| L □ | |
| D □ | |
| S □ | |

**NOTES**

# daily journal

**WHAT WENT WELL YESTERDAY?**

**WHAT WENT POORLY YESTERDAY?**

**WHAT CAN I IMPROVE?**

**ON MY MIND TODAY...**

_____

_____

_____

_____

_____

_____

_____

_____

_____

_____

_____

_____

_____

_____

# daily plan

**AFFIRMATION**

**SLEEP**

.................................................

**WATER**

1  2  3  4  5  6  7  8  9  10

.................................................

**GOALS**

**EXERCISE**

| 24 HOUR PLAN | ACTUAL |
|:---:|:---:|

**B** ☐

.................................................

**L** ☐

.................................................

**D** ☐

.................................................

**S** ☐

**NOTES**

# daily journal

**WHAT WENT WELL YESTERDAY?**

**WHAT WENT POORLY YESTERDAY?**

**WHAT CAN I IMPROVE?**

**ON MY MIND TODAY...**

_____

_____

_____

_____

_____

_____

_____

_____

_____

_____

_____

_____

_____

# daily plan

DATE

| AFFIRMATION | SLEEP |
| | WATER |
| | 1  2  3  4  5  6  7  8  9  10 |
| GOALS | EXERCISE |

| 24 HOUR PLAN | ACTUAL |
|---|---|
| B | |
| L | |
| D | |
| S | |

NOTES

# daily journal

**WHAT WENT WELL YESTERDAY?**

**WHAT WENT POORLY YESTERDAY?**

**WHAT CAN I IMPROVE?**

**ON MY MIND TODAY...**

_____
_____
_____
_____
_____
_____
_____
_____
_____
_____
_____
_____
_____

# daily plan

| AFFIRMATION | SLEEP |
|---|---|
| | WATER |
| | 1 2 3 4 5 6 7 8 9 10 |
| GOALS | EXERCISE |

| 24 HOUR PLAN | ACTUAL |
|---|---|
| B ☐ | |
| L ☐ | |
| D ☐ | |
| S ☐ | |

NOTES

# daily journal

**WHAT WENT WELL YESTERDAY?**

**WHAT WENT POORLY YESTERDAY?**

**WHAT CAN I IMPROVE?**

**ON MY MIND TODAY...**

_____
_____
_____
_____
_____
_____
_____
_____
_____
_____
_____
_____
_____

# daily plan

DATE

**AFFIRMATION**

**SLEEP**

**WATER**

1 2 3 4 5 6 7 8 9 10

**GOALS**

**EXERCISE**

| 24 HOUR PLAN | ACTUAL |
|---|---|
| B | |
| L | |
| D | |
| S | |

**NOTES**

# daily journal

**WHAT WENT WELL YESTERDAY?**

**WHAT WENT POORLY YESTERDAY?**

**WHAT CAN I IMPROVE?**

**ON MY MIND TODAY...**

_____
_____
_____
_____
_____
_____
_____
_____
_____
_____
_____
_____
_____

# daily plan

DATE

**AFFIRMATION**

**SLEEP**

**WATER**

1 2 3 4 5 6 7 8 9 10

**GOALS**

**EXERCISE**

| 24 HOUR PLAN | ACTUAL |
|---|---|
| B | |
| L | |
| D | |
| S | |

**NOTES**

# daily journal

**WHAT WENT WELL YESTERDAY?**

**WHAT WENT POORLY YESTERDAY?**

**WHAT CAN I IMPROVE?**

**ON MY MIND TODAY...**

_____
_____
_____
_____
_____
_____
_____
_____
_____
_____
_____
_____
_____
_____

# daily plan

DATE

| AFFIRMATION | SLEEP |
| | WATER |
| | 1 2 3 4 5 6 7 8 9 10 |
| GOALS | EXERCISE |

| 24 HOUR PLAN | ACTUAL |
|---|---|
| B | ☐ |
| L | ☐ |
| D | ☐ |
| S | ☐ |

NOTES

# daily journal

**WHAT WENT WELL YESTERDAY?**

**WHAT WENT POORLY YESTERDAY?**

**WHAT CAN I IMPROVE?**

**ON MY MIND TODAY...**

_____
_____
_____
_____
_____
_____
_____
_____
_____
_____
_____
_____
_____
_____
_____

# daily plan

**AFFIRMATION**

**SLEEP**

**WATER**

1 2 3 4 5 6 7 8 9 10

**GOALS**

**EXERCISE**

| 24 HOUR PLAN | ACTUAL |
|:---:|:---:|
| B ☐ | |
| L ☐ | |
| D ☐ | |
| S ☐ | |

**NOTES**

# daily journal

**WHAT WENT WELL YESTERDAY?**

**WHAT WENT POORLY YESTERDAY?**

**WHAT CAN I IMPROVE?**

**ON MY MIND TODAY...**

_____

_____

_____

_____

_____

_____

_____

_____

_____

_____

_____

_____

_____

# daily plan

**AFFIRMATION**

**SLEEP**

**WATER**

1 2 3 4 5 6 7 8 9 10

**GOALS**

**EXERCISE**

| 24 HOUR PLAN | ACTUAL |
|---|---|
| **B** | ☐ |
| **L** | ☐ |
| **D** | ☐ |
| **S** | ☐ |

**NOTES**

# daily journal

**WHAT WENT WELL YESTERDAY?**

**WHAT WENT POORLY YESTERDAY?**

**WHAT CAN I IMPROVE?**

**ON MY MIND TODAY...**

_____
_____
_____
_____
_____
_____
_____
_____
_____
_____
_____
_____
_____

# daily plan

DATE

| AFFIRMATION | SLEEP |
| | WATER |
| | 1 2 3 4 5 6 7 8 9 10 |
| GOALS | EXERCISE |

| 24 HOUR PLAN | ACTUAL |
|---|---|
| B ☐ | |
| L ☐ | |
| D ☐ | |
| S ☐ | |

NOTES

# daily journal

**WHAT WENT WELL YESTERDAY?**

**WHAT WENT POORLY YESTERDAY?**

**WHAT CAN I IMPROVE?**

## ON MY MIND TODAY...

# daily plan

DATE

**AFFIRMATION**

**SLEEP**

**WATER**

1 2 3 4 5 6 7 8 9 10

**GOALS**

**EXERCISE**

| 24 HOUR PLAN | ACTUAL |
|---|---|
| B | |
| L | |
| D | |
| S | |

**NOTES**

# daily journal

**WHAT WENT WELL YESTERDAY?**

**WHAT WENT POORLY YESTERDAY?**

**WHAT CAN I IMPROVE?**

**ON MY MIND TODAY...**

_____

_____

_____

_____

_____

_____

_____

_____

_____

_____

_____

_____

_____

# daily plan

DATE

**AFFIRMATION**

**SLEEP**

**WATER**

1 2 3 4 5 6 7 8 9 10

**GOALS**

**EXERCISE**

| 24 HOUR PLAN | ACTUAL |
|---|---|
| B | |
| L | |
| D | |
| S | |

**NOTES**

# daily journal

**WHAT WENT WELL YESTERDAY?**

**WHAT WENT POORLY YESTERDAY?**

**WHAT CAN I IMPROVE?**

**ON MY MIND TODAY...**

_____
_____
_____
_____
_____
_____
_____
_____
_____
_____
_____
_____
_____
_____

# daily plan

**DATE**

**AFFIRMATION**

**SLEEP**

**WATER**

1 2 3 4 5 6 7 8 9 10

**GOALS**

**EXERCISE**

| 24 HOUR PLAN | ACTUAL |
|---|---|
| B | |
| L | |
| D | |
| S | |

**NOTES**

# daily journal

**WHAT WENT WELL YESTERDAY?**

**WHAT WENT POORLY YESTERDAY?**

**WHAT CAN I IMPROVE?**

**ON MY MIND TODAY...**

_____
_____
_____
_____
_____
_____
_____
_____
_____
_____
_____
_____
_____

# daily plan

DATE

## AFFIRMATION

## SLEEP

......................................................

## WATER

1 2 3 4 5 6 7 8 9 10

......................................................

## GOALS

## EXERCISE

| 24 HOUR PLAN | ACTUAL |
|---|---|
| B ☐ | |
| L ☐ | |
| D ☐ | |
| S ☐ | |

## NOTES

# daily journal

**WHAT WENT WELL YESTERDAY?**

**WHAT WENT POORLY YESTERDAY?**

**WHAT CAN I IMPROVE?**

**ON MY MIND TODAY...**

_____
_____
_____
_____
_____
_____
_____
_____
_____
_____
_____
_____
_____

# daily plan

| AFFIRMATION | SLEEP |
| --- | --- |
| | **WATER** |
| | 1  2  3  4  5  6  7  8  9  10 |
| **GOALS** | **EXERCISE** |

| 24 HOUR PLAN | ACTUAL |
| --- | --- |
| **B** ☐ | |
| **L** ☐ | |
| **D** ☐ | |
| **S** ☐ | |

**NOTES**

# daily journal

**WHAT WENT WELL YESTERDAY?**

**WHAT WENT POORLY YESTERDAY?**

**WHAT CAN I IMPROVE?**

**ON MY MIND TODAY...**

_____
_____
_____
_____
_____
_____
_____
_____
_____
_____
_____
_____
_____

# daily plan

DATE

| AFFIRMATION | SLEEP |
| | WATER |
| | 1 2 3 4 5 6 7 8 9 10 |
| GOALS | EXERCISE |

| 24 HOUR PLAN | ACTUAL |
| --- | --- |
| B | ☐ |
| L | ☐ |
| D | ☐ |
| S | ☐ |

NOTES

# daily journal

**WHAT WENT WELL YESTERDAY?**

**WHAT WENT POORLY YESTERDAY?**

**WHAT CAN I IMPROVE?**

**ON MY MIND TODAY...**

# daily plan

DATE

**AFFIRMATION**

**SLEEP**

**WATER**

1 2 3 4 5 6 7 8 9 10

**GOALS**

**EXERCISE**

| 24 HOUR PLAN | ACTUAL |
|---|---|
| B ☐ | |
| L ☐ | |
| D ☐ | |
| S ☐ | |

**NOTES**

# daily journal

**WHAT WENT WELL YESTERDAY?**

**WHAT WENT POORLY YESTERDAY?**

**WHAT CAN I IMPROVE?**

**ON MY MIND TODAY...**

_____
_____
_____
_____
_____
_____
_____
_____
_____
_____
_____
_____
_____
_____

# daily plan

DATE

**AFFIRMATION**

**SLEEP**

**WATER**

1 2 3 4 5 6 7 8 9 10

**GOALS**

**EXERCISE**

| 24 HOUR PLAN | ACTUAL |
|:---:|:---:|
| B | |
| L | |
| D | |
| S | |

**NOTES**

# daily journal

**WHAT WENT WELL YESTERDAY?**

**WHAT WENT POORLY YESTERDAY?**

**WHAT CAN I IMPROVE?**

**ON MY MIND TODAY...**

_____

_____

_____

_____

_____

_____

_____

_____

_____

_____

_____

_____

_____

_____

# daily plan

DATE

**AFFIRMATION**

**SLEEP**

**WATER**

1 2 3 4 5 6 7 8 9 10

**GOALS**

**EXERCISE**

| 24 HOUR PLAN | ACTUAL |
|---|---|
| B | ☐ |
| L | ☐ |
| D | ☐ |
| S | ☐ |

**NOTES**

# daily journal

**WHAT WENT WELL YESTERDAY?**

**WHAT WENT POORLY YESTERDAY?**

**WHAT CAN I IMPROVE?**

**ON MY MIND TODAY...**

# daily plan

**DATE**

| AFFIRMATION | SLEEP |
| --- | --- |
| | **WATER** |
| | 1  2  3  4  5  6  7  8  9  10 |
| **GOALS** | **EXERCISE** |

| 24 HOUR PLAN | ACTUAL |
| --- | --- |
| B ☐ | |
| L ☐ | |
| D ☐ | |
| S ☐ | |

**NOTES**

# daily journal

**WHAT WENT WELL YESTERDAY?**

**WHAT WENT POORLY YESTERDAY?**

**WHAT CAN I IMPROVE?**

**ON MY MIND TODAY...**

_____
_____
_____
_____
_____
_____
_____
_____
_____
_____
_____
_____
_____
_____

# daily plan

**AFFIRMATION**

**SLEEP**

**WATER**

1 2 3 4 5 6 7 8 9 10

**GOALS**

**EXERCISE**

| 24 HOUR PLAN | ACTUAL |
|:---:|:---:|
| B | |
| L | |
| D | |
| S | |

**NOTES**

# daily journal

**WHAT WENT WELL YESTERDAY?**

**WHAT WENT POORLY YESTERDAY?**

**WHAT CAN I IMPROVE?**

**ON MY MIND TODAY...**

_____

_____

_____

_____

_____

_____

_____

_____

_____

_____

_____

_____

_____

# daily plan

DATE

| AFFIRMATION | SLEEP |
| | WATER |
| | 1 2 3 4 5 6 7 8 9 10 |
| GOALS | EXERCISE |

| 24 HOUR PLAN | ACTUAL |
| --- | --- |
| B ☐ | |
| L ☐ | |
| D ☐ | |
| S ☐ | |

NOTES

# daily journal

**WHAT WENT WELL YESTERDAY?**

**WHAT WENT POORLY YESTERDAY?**

**WHAT CAN I IMPROVE?**

**ON MY MIND TODAY...**

_____
_____
_____
_____
_____
_____
_____
_____
_____
_____
_____
_____
_____
_____

# daily plan

**DATE**

**AFFIRMATION**

**SLEEP**

**WATER**

1 2 3 4 5 6 7 8 9 10

**GOALS**

**EXERCISE**

| 24 HOUR PLAN | ACTUAL |
|:---:|:---:|
| B | |
| L | |
| D | |
| S | |

**NOTES**

# daily journal

**WHAT WENT WELL YESTERDAY?**

**WHAT WENT POORLY YESTERDAY?**

**WHAT CAN I IMPROVE?**

**ON MY MIND TODAY...**

_____

_____

_____

_____

_____

_____

_____

_____

_____

_____

_____

_____

_____

_____

# daily plan

**AFFIRMATION**

**SLEEP**

**WATER**

1 2 3 4 5 6 7 8 9 10

**GOALS**

**EXERCISE**

| 24 HOUR PLAN | ACTUAL |
|---|---|
| **B** ☐ | |
| **L** ☐ | |
| **D** ☐ | |
| **S** ☐ | |

**NOTES**

# daily journal

**WHAT WENT WELL YESTERDAY?**

**WHAT WENT POORLY YESTERDAY?**

**WHAT CAN I IMPROVE?**

**ON MY MIND TODAY...**

_____

_____

_____

_____

_____

_____

_____

_____

_____

_____

_____

_____

_____

# daily plan

DATE

**AFFIRMATION**

**SLEEP**

**WATER**

1 2 3 4 5 6 7 8 9 10

**GOALS**

**EXERCISE**

| 24 HOUR PLAN | ACTUAL |
|---|---|
| B | |
| L | |
| D | |
| S | |

**NOTES**

# daily journal

**WHAT WENT WELL YESTERDAY?**

**WHAT WENT POORLY YESTERDAY?**

**WHAT CAN I IMPROVE?**

## ON MY MIND TODAY...

# daily plan

DATE

| AFFIRMATION | SLEEP |
| | WATER |
| | 1  2  3  4  5  6  7  8  9  10 |
| GOALS | EXERCISE |

| 24 HOUR PLAN | ACTUAL |
|---|---|
| B | ☐ |
| L | ☐ |
| D | ☐ |
| S | ☐ |

NOTES

# daily journal

**WHAT WENT WELL YESTERDAY?**

**WHAT WENT POORLY YESTERDAY?**

**WHAT CAN I IMPROVE?**

**ON MY MIND TODAY...**

_____
_____
_____
_____
_____
_____
_____
_____
_____
_____
_____
_____
_____

# daily plan

DATE

| AFFIRMATION | SLEEP |
| | WATER |
| | 1 2 3 4 5 6 7 8 9 10 |
| GOALS | EXERCISE |

| 24 HOUR PLAN | ACTUAL |
|---|---|
| B | |
| L | |
| D | |
| S | |

NOTES

# daily journal

**WHAT WENT WELL YESTERDAY?**

**WHAT WENT POORLY YESTERDAY?**

**WHAT CAN I IMPROVE?**

**ON MY MIND TODAY...**

_____
_____
_____
_____
_____
_____
_____
_____
_____
_____
_____
_____
_____

# daily plan

DATE

**AFFIRMATION**

**SLEEP**

**WATER**

1 2 3 4 5 6 7 8 9 10

**GOALS**

**EXERCISE**

| 24 HOUR PLAN | ACTUAL |
|---|---|
| B | |
| L | |
| D | |
| S | |

**NOTES**

# daily journal

**WHAT WENT WELL YESTERDAY?**

**WHAT WENT POORLY YESTERDAY?**

**WHAT CAN I IMPROVE?**

**ON MY MIND TODAY...**

_____
_____
_____
_____
_____
_____
_____
_____
_____
_____
_____
_____
_____
_____

# daily plan

**DATE**

| AFFIRMATION | SLEEP |
| --- | --- |
| | **WATER** |
| | 1  2  3  4  5  6  7  8  9  10 |
| **GOALS** | **EXERCISE** |

| 24 HOUR PLAN | ACTUAL |
| --- | --- |
| **B** | ☐ |
| **L** | ☐ |
| **D** | ☐ |
| **S** | ☐ |

**NOTES**

# daily journal

**WHAT WENT WELL YESTERDAY?**

**WHAT WENT POORLY YESTERDAY?**

**WHAT CAN I IMPROVE?**

**ON MY MIND TODAY...**

# daily plan

DATE

**AFFIRMATION**

**SLEEP**

**WATER**

1 2 3 4 5 6 7 8 9 10

**GOALS**

**EXERCISE**

| 24 HOUR PLAN | ACTUAL |
|---|---|
| B | |
| L | |
| D | |
| S | |

**NOTES**

# daily journal

**WHAT WENT WELL YESTERDAY?**

**WHAT WENT POORLY YESTERDAY?**

**WHAT CAN I IMPROVE?**

**ON MY MIND TODAY...**

_____

_____

_____

_____

_____

_____

_____

_____

_____

_____

_____

_____

_____

_____

# daily plan

| AFFIRMATION | SLEEP |
|---|---|
| | WATER |
| | 1  2  3  4  5  6  7  8  9  10 |
| GOALS | EXERCISE |

| 24 HOUR PLAN | ACTUAL |
|---|---|
| B | |
| L | |
| D | |
| S | |

NOTES

# daily journal

**WHAT WENT WELL YESTERDAY?**

**WHAT WENT POORLY YESTERDAY?**

**WHAT CAN I IMPROVE?**

**ON MY MIND TODAY...**

_____

_____

_____

_____

_____

_____

_____

_____

_____

_____

_____

_____

_____

# daily plan

DATE

**AFFIRMATION**

**SLEEP**

**WATER**

1 2 3 4 5 6 7 8 9 10

**GOALS**

**EXERCISE**

| 24 HOUR PLAN | ACTUAL |
|---|---|
| B | |
| L | |
| D | |
| S | |

**NOTES**

# daily journal

**WHAT WENT WELL YESTERDAY?**

**WHAT WENT POORLY YESTERDAY?**

**WHAT CAN I IMPROVE?**

## ON MY MIND TODAY...

_____

_____

_____

_____

_____

_____

_____

_____

_____

_____

_____

_____

# daily plan

DATE

| AFFIRMATION | SLEEP |
| --- | --- |
| | WATER |
| | 1 2 3 4 5 6 7 8 9 10 |
| GOALS | EXERCISE |

| 24 HOUR PLAN | ACTUAL |
| --- | --- |
| B | |
| L | |
| D | |
| S | |

NOTES

# daily journal

**WHAT WENT WELL YESTERDAY?**

**WHAT WENT POORLY YESTERDAY?**

**WHAT CAN I IMPROVE?**

**ON MY MIND TODAY...**

_____
_____
_____
_____
_____
_____
_____
_____
_____
_____
_____
_____
_____

# daily plan

DATE

| AFFIRMATION | SLEEP |
|---|---|
| | WATER |
| | 1 2 3 4 5 6 7 8 9 10 |
| GOALS | EXERCISE |

| 24 HOUR PLAN | ACTUAL |
|---|---|
| B | |
| L | |
| D | |
| S | |

NOTES

# daily journal

**WHAT WENT WELL YESTERDAY?**

**WHAT WENT POORLY YESTERDAY?**

**WHAT CAN I IMPROVE?**

## ON MY MIND TODAY...

_____
_____
_____
_____
_____
_____
_____
_____
_____
_____
_____
_____
_____

# daily plan

DATE

AFFIRMATION

SLEEP

WATER

1 2 3 4 5 6 7 8 9 10

GOALS

EXERCISE

| 24 HOUR PLAN | ACTUAL |
|---|---|
| B □ | |
| L □ | |
| D □ | |
| S □ | |

NOTES

# daily journal

**WHAT WENT WELL YESTERDAY?**

**WHAT WENT POORLY YESTERDAY?**

**WHAT CAN I IMPROVE?**

**ON MY MIND TODAY...**

_____
_____
_____
_____
_____
_____
_____
_____
_____
_____
_____
_____
_____

# daily plan

**DATE**

**AFFIRMATION**

**SLEEP**

**WATER**

1 2 3 4 5 6 7 8 9 10

**GOALS**

**EXERCISE**

| 24 HOUR PLAN | ACTUAL |
|---|---|
| B | |
| L | |
| D | |
| S | |

**NOTES**

# daily journal

**WHAT WENT WELL YESTERDAY?**

**WHAT WENT POORLY YESTERDAY?**

**WHAT CAN I IMPROVE?**

## ON MY MIND TODAY...

_____
_____
_____
_____
_____
_____
_____
_____
_____
_____
_____
_____

# daily plan

**DATE**

| AFFIRMATION | SLEEP |
| --- | --- |
| | **WATER** |
| | 1 2 3 4 5 6 7 8 9 10 |
| **GOALS** | **EXERCISE** |

| 24 HOUR PLAN | ACTUAL |
| --- | --- |
| **B** | □ |
| **L** | □ |
| **D** | □ |
| **S** | □ |

**NOTES**

# daily journal

**WHAT WENT WELL YESTERDAY?**

**WHAT WENT POORLY YESTERDAY?**

**WHAT CAN I IMPROVE?**

**ON MY MIND TODAY...**

# daily plan

DATE

| AFFIRMATION | SLEEP |
| --- | --- |
| | WATER |
| | 1 2 3 4 5 6 7 8 9 10 |
| GOALS | EXERCISE |

| 24 HOUR PLAN | ACTUAL |
| --- | --- |
| B | ☐ |
| L | ☐ |
| D | ☐ |
| S | ☐ |

NOTES

# daily journal

**WHAT WENT WELL YESTERDAY?**

**WHAT WENT POORLY YESTERDAY?**

**WHAT CAN I IMPROVE?**

**ON MY MIND TODAY...**

_____
_____
_____
_____
_____
_____
_____
_____
_____
_____
_____
_____

# daily plan

DATE

| AFFIRMATION | SLEEP |
| | WATER |
| | 1 2 3 4 5 6 7 8 9 10 |
| GOALS | EXERCISE |

| 24 HOUR PLAN | ACTUAL |
|---|---|
| B ☐ | |
| L ☐ | |
| D ☐ | |
| S ☐ | |

NOTES

# daily journal

**WHAT WENT WELL YESTERDAY?**

**WHAT WENT POORLY YESTERDAY?**

**WHAT CAN I IMPROVE?**

**ON MY MIND TODAY...**

_____

_____

_____

_____

_____

_____

_____

_____

_____

_____

_____

_____

# daily plan

DATE

| AFFIRMATION | SLEEP |
| --- | --- |
| | WATER |
| | 1  2  3  4  5  6  7  8  9  10 |
| GOALS | EXERCISE |

| 24 HOUR PLAN | ACTUAL |
| --- | --- |
| B | |
| L | |
| D | |
| S | |

NOTES

# daily journal

**WHAT WENT WELL YESTERDAY?**

**WHAT WENT POORLY YESTERDAY?**

**WHAT CAN I IMPROVE?**

**ON MY MIND TODAY...**

_____
_____
_____
_____
_____
_____
_____
_____
_____
_____
_____
_____

# daily plan

DATE

**AFFIRMATION**

**SLEEP**

**WATER**

1 2 3 4 5 6 7 8 9 10

**GOALS**

**EXERCISE**

| 24 HOUR PLAN | ACTUAL |
|---|---|
| B | |
| L | |
| D | |
| S | |

**NOTES**

# daily journal

**WHAT WENT WELL YESTERDAY?**

**WHAT WENT POORLY YESTERDAY?**

**WHAT CAN I IMPROVE?**

**ON MY MIND TODAY...**

_____

_____

_____

_____

_____

_____

_____

_____

_____

_____

_____

_____

_____

# daily plan

DATE

| AFFIRMATION | SLEEP |
| | WATER |
| | 1 2 3 4 5 6 7 8 9 10 |
| GOALS | EXERCISE |

| 24 HOUR PLAN | ACTUAL |
|---|---|
| B | |
| L | |
| D | |
| S | |

NOTES

# daily journal

**WHAT WENT WELL YESTERDAY?**

**WHAT WENT POORLY YESTERDAY?**

**WHAT CAN I IMPROVE?**

**ON MY MIND TODAY...**

_____
_____
_____
_____
_____
_____
_____
_____
_____
_____
_____
_____
_____

# daily plan

DATE

| AFFIRMATION | SLEEP |
| --- | --- |
| | WATER |
| | 1 2 3 4 5 6 7 8 9 10 |
| GOALS | EXERCISE |
| | |

| 24 HOUR PLAN | ACTUAL |
| --- | --- |
| B ☐ | |
| L ☐ | |
| D ☐ | |
| S ☐ | |

NOTES

# daily journal

**WHAT WENT WELL YESTERDAY?**

**WHAT WENT POORLY YESTERDAY?**

**WHAT CAN I IMPROVE?**

## ON MY MIND TODAY...

_____
_____
_____
_____
_____
_____
_____
_____
_____
_____
_____
_____
_____
_____

# daily plan

DATE

| AFFIRMATION | SLEEP |
| | |
| | WATER |
| | 1 2 3 4 5 6 7 8 9 10 |
| GOALS | EXERCISE |
| | |

| 24 HOUR PLAN | ACTUAL |
| --- | --- |
| B | |
| L | |
| D | |
| S | |

NOTES

# daily journal

**WHAT WENT WELL YESTERDAY?**

**WHAT WENT POORLY YESTERDAY?**

**WHAT CAN I IMPROVE?**

**ON MY MIND TODAY...**

_____
_____
_____
_____
_____
_____
_____
_____
_____
_____
_____
_____
_____
_____

# daily plan

**DATE**

| AFFIRMATION | SLEEP |
| --- | --- |
| | WATER |
| | 1 2 3 4 5 6 7 8 9 10 |
| GOALS | EXERCISE |

| 24 HOUR PLAN | ACTUAL |
| --- | --- |
| B | |
| L | |
| D | |
| S | |

**NOTES**

# daily journal

## WHAT WENT WELL YESTERDAY?

## WHAT WENT POORLY YESTERDAY?

## WHAT CAN I IMPROVE?

## ON MY MIND TODAY...

_____
_____
_____
_____
_____
_____
_____
_____
_____
_____
_____
_____
_____

# daily plan

**DATE**

| AFFIRMATION | SLEEP |
| --- | --- |
| | **WATER** |
| | 1 2 3 4 5 6 7 8 9 10 |
| **GOALS** | **EXERCISE** |

| 24 HOUR PLAN | ACTUAL |
| --- | --- |
| B | |
| L | |
| D | |
| S | |

**NOTES**

# daily journal

**WHAT WENT WELL YESTERDAY?**

**WHAT WENT POORLY YESTERDAY?**

**WHAT CAN I IMPROVE?**

**ON MY MIND TODAY...**

# daily plan

DATE

**AFFIRMATION**

**SLEEP**

**WATER**

1 2 3 4 5 6 7 8 9 10

**GOALS**

**EXERCISE**

| 24 HOUR PLAN | ACTUAL |
|---|---|
| B | |
| L | |
| D | |
| S | |

**NOTES**

# daily journal

**WHAT WENT WELL YESTERDAY?**

**WHAT WENT POORLY YESTERDAY?**

**WHAT CAN I IMPROVE?**

**ON MY MIND TODAY...**

_____
_____
_____
_____
_____
_____
_____
_____
_____
_____
_____
_____
_____
_____

# daily plan

DATE

AFFIRMATION

SLEEP

WATER

1 2 3 4 5 6 7 8 9 10

GOALS

EXERCISE

| 24 HOUR PLAN | ACTUAL |
|---|---|
| B | |
| L | |
| D | |
| S | |

NOTES

# daily journal

**WHAT WENT WELL YESTERDAY?**

**WHAT WENT POORLY YESTERDAY?**

**WHAT CAN I IMPROVE?**

**ON MY MIND TODAY...**

_____

_____

_____

_____

_____

_____

_____

_____

_____

_____

_____

_____

_____

# daily plan

**DATE**

| AFFIRMATION | SLEEP |
| | WATER |
| | 1 2 3 4 5 6 7 8 9 10 |
| GOALS | EXERCISE |

| 24 HOUR PLAN | ACTUAL |
|---|---|
| B | |
| L | |
| D | |
| S | |

**NOTES**

# daily journal

**WHAT WENT WELL YESTERDAY?**

**WHAT WENT POORLY YESTERDAY?**

**WHAT CAN I IMPROVE?**

**ON MY MIND TODAY...**

_____
_____
_____
_____
_____
_____
_____
_____
_____
_____
_____
_____
_____

# daily plan

DATE

## AFFIRMATION

## SLEEP

## WATER

1 2 3 4 5 6 7 8 9 10

## GOALS

## EXERCISE

| 24 HOUR PLAN | ACTUAL |
|---|---|
| B | |
| L | |
| D | |
| S | |

## NOTES

# daily journal

**WHAT WENT WELL YESTERDAY?**


**WHAT WENT POORLY YESTERDAY?**


**WHAT CAN I IMPROVE?**


## ON MY MIND TODAY...

_____

_____

_____

_____

_____

_____

_____

_____

_____

_____

_____

_____

# daily plan

DATE

**AFFIRMATION**

**SLEEP**

**WATER**

1 2 3 4 5 6 7 8 9 10

**GOALS**

**EXERCISE**

| 24 HOUR PLAN | ACTUAL |
|---|---|
| B | |
| L | |
| D | |
| S | |

**NOTES**

# daily journal

**WHAT WENT WELL YESTERDAY?**

**WHAT WENT POORLY YESTERDAY?**

**WHAT CAN I IMPROVE?**

**ON MY MIND TODAY...**

_____
_____
_____
_____
_____
_____
_____
_____
_____
_____
_____
_____
_____

# daily plan

DATE

| AFFIRMATION | SLEEP |
|---|---|
| | WATER |
| | 1 2 3 4 5 6 7 8 9 10 |
| GOALS | EXERCISE |
| | |

| 24 HOUR PLAN | ACTUAL |
|---|---|
| B | |
| L | |
| D | |
| S | |

NOTES

# daily journal

**WHAT WENT WELL YESTERDAY?**


**WHAT WENT POORLY YESTERDAY?**


**WHAT CAN I IMPROVE?**


**ON MY MIND TODAY...**

_____
_____
_____
_____
_____
_____
_____
_____
_____
_____
_____
_____

# daily plan

DATE

| AFFIRMATION | SLEEP |
| | |

| | WATER |
| | 1 2 3 4 5 6 7 8 9 10 |

| GOALS | EXERCISE |

| 24 HOUR PLAN | ACTUAL |
| --- | --- |
| B | □ |
| L | □ |
| D | □ |
| S | □ |

NOTES

# daily journal

**WHAT WENT WELL YESTERDAY?**

**WHAT WENT POORLY YESTERDAY?**

**WHAT CAN I IMPROVE?**

## ON MY MIND TODAY...

_____
_____
_____
_____
_____
_____
_____
_____
_____
_____
_____
_____
_____
_____

# daily plan

DATE

**AFFIRMATION**

**SLEEP**

**WATER**

1 2 3 4 5 6 7 8 9 10

**GOALS**

**EXERCISE**

| 24 HOUR PLAN | ACTUAL |
|---|---|
| B | |
| L | |
| D | |
| S | |

**NOTES**

# daily journal

**WHAT WENT WELL YESTERDAY?**

**WHAT WENT POORLY YESTERDAY?**

**WHAT CAN I IMPROVE?**

**ON MY MIND TODAY...**

_____
_____
_____
_____
_____
_____
_____
_____
_____
_____
_____
_____
_____
_____

# daily plan

DATE

**AFFIRMATION**

**SLEEP**

**WATER**

1  2  3  4  5  6  7  8  9  10

**GOALS**

**EXERCISE**

| 24 HOUR PLAN | ACTUAL |
|:---:|:---:|
| B | |
| L | |
| D | |
| S | |

**NOTES**

# daily journal

**WHAT WENT WELL YESTERDAY?**

**WHAT WENT POORLY YESTERDAY?**

**WHAT CAN I IMPROVE?**

**ON MY MIND TODAY...**

_____
_____
_____
_____
_____
_____
_____
_____
_____
_____
_____
_____
_____

# daily plan

DATE

| AFFIRMATION | SLEEP |
| | WATER |
| | 1 2 3 4 5 6 7 8 9 10 |
| GOALS | EXERCISE |

| 24 HOUR PLAN | ACTUAL |
| --- | --- |
| B | |
| L | |
| D | |
| S | |

NOTES

# daily journal

**WHAT WENT WELL YESTERDAY?**

**WHAT WENT POORLY YESTERDAY?**

**WHAT CAN I IMPROVE?**

**ON MY MIND TODAY...**

# daily plan

**DATE**

**AFFIRMATION**

**SLEEP**

**WATER**

1 2 3 4 5 6 7 8 9 10

**GOALS**

**EXERCISE**

| 24 HOUR PLAN | ACTUAL |
|---|---|
| B | |
| L | |
| D | |
| S | |

**NOTES**

# daily journal

**WHAT WENT WELL YESTERDAY?**

**WHAT WENT POORLY YESTERDAY?**

**WHAT CAN I IMPROVE?**

**ON MY MIND TODAY...**

_____
_____
_____
_____
_____
_____
_____
_____
_____
_____
_____
_____
_____
_____

# daily plan

DATE

| AFFIRMATION | SLEEP |
| | WATER |
| | 1 2 3 4 5 6 7 8 9 10 |
| GOALS | EXERCISE |

| 24 HOUR PLAN | ACTUAL |
|---|---|
| B | |
| L | |
| D | |
| S | |

NOTES

# daily journal

**WHAT WENT WELL YESTERDAY?**

**WHAT WENT POORLY YESTERDAY?**

**WHAT CAN I IMPROVE?**

**ON MY MIND TODAY...**

_____
_____
_____
_____
_____
_____
_____
_____
_____
_____
_____
_____
_____

# daily plan

**DATE**

| AFFIRMATION | SLEEP |
|---|---|
| | **WATER** |
| | 1  2  3  4  5  6  7  8  9  10 |
| **GOALS** | **EXERCISE** |

| 24 HOUR PLAN | ACTUAL |
|---|---|
| B | ☐ |
| L | ☐ |
| D | ☐ |
| S | ☐ |

**NOTES**

# daily journal

WHAT WENT WELL YESTERDAY?

WHAT WENT POORLY YESTERDAY?

WHAT CAN I IMPROVE?

ON MY MIND TODAY...

_____
_____
_____
_____
_____
_____
_____
_____
_____
_____
_____
_____
_____
_____

# daily plan

DATE

| AFFIRMATION | SLEEP |
| --- | --- |
| | WATER |
| | 1 2 3 4 5 6 7 8 9 10 |
| GOALS | EXERCISE |

| 24 HOUR PLAN | ACTUAL |
| --- | --- |
| B | |
| L | |
| D | |
| S | |

NOTES

Made in the USA
Columbia, SC
13 October 2020